Delivered by
JESUS

J. L. ZOTOS

Trilogy Christian Publishers
A Wholly Owned Subsidiary of Trinity Broadcasting Network
2442 Michelle Drive
Tustin, CA 92780

For information, address Trilogy Christian Publishing
Rights Department, 2442 Michelle Drive, Tustin, Ca 92780.
Trilogy Christian Publishing/ TBN and colophon are trademarks of Trinity Broadcasting Network.

For information about special discounts for bulk purchases, please contact Trilogy Christian Publishing.

Manufactured in the United States of America

10 9 8 7 6 5 4 3 2 1

Library of Congress Cataloging-in-Publication Data is available.

ISBN 978-1-64088-983-5 (Print Book)
ISBN 978-1-64088-984-2 (ebook)

To the Lord Jesus Christ. He came and went
to the cross and set me free, and since I have
met him, I have never been the same.

CONTENTS

Acknowledgment 7

Chapter 1: Meeting the King of Kings 9

Chapter 2: Childhood....................................15

Chapter 3: Adolescence................................20

Chapter 4: Teenager....................................26

Chapter 5: My Dad.....................................33

Chapter 6: Homosexual Living 38

Chapter 7: Going For God 45

Chapter 8: The Word of God 50

Chapter 9: Mom...56

Chapter 10: My Foundation 65

ACKNOWLEDGMENT

I acknowledge Pastor Robb and Linda Thompson for never giving up on me and praying for me, not letting me go when I failed the Father. They taught me the Word and walked it out in front of me uncompromised. They are my spiritual parents forever.

CHAPTER 1

Meeting the King of Kings

I asked the Lord in to my heart in April of 1980. I had left my significant other because of an argument over marijuana. I did not let anyone tell me if I could buy it, smoke it, or eat it if I wanted. I had put everything I owned in a 1971 Chevy Impala, which is pretty much a boat. You could easily put six people in the trunk quite comfortably. In a matter of about twenty minutes, I packed it all up and left. It was about 7:00 p.m. at night.

I was pretty angry, and there was no talking me out of it. I really wish that I would have known then how what we do affects everyone around us and really cared how it affected them. I drove four hours to Cicero, Illinois. I went to one of my sister's homes. Her name is Jackie; she had always been my ark.

Jackie took over the best she could when we were kids. She is only three years older than I am, but she always had that mommy instinct, and she kind of had to 'cause our parents just did not know the Lord; and they did not really do what they needed to for Jackie. And I, I am the youngest of seven. Jackie and I were from my dad. The first five kids were from my mom's first marriage. I always ran to Jackie, and she always took me in and took care of me. I went to her home, and the next morning, I was seriously depressed.

I hated my life. I hated what I was, or maybe I hated how I ended up that way. I was going to take my life. I was not going to leave a note. I was just going to do it. You see, by now, I was seeing the act. You see, once you start seeing it, that picture ministers to you. I kept seeing myself put a knife in my heart, and all the pain would just go away—the pain of a child that had been taken from all her life. They took my childhood, my womanhood, and so much more. My step-dad, his name was Bob, began molesting me at age 4.5. My brother started molesting me when I was 5. Walter did not have as much access to me as my stepdad because he was not around as much, but he also molested me when he had me alone. I had no one to watch over me.

My dad was an alcoholic and worked at another business he was running. My mom was working a lot, running our tavern, and she was always working or with the man that took the most from me. Anyway, Jackie and her husband went to work that morning; and they were gone most of the day. I remember knowing I was going to do this. Then I was sitting there, and the front doorbell rang. I opened the door, and there stood one of my older sisters whom I had not seen in at least three years, and she has a woman with her who had introduced her to Jesus. I had no idea they were coming over. And get this, they came in and sat down and told me the Lord sent them there. Now for me, the question was: the Lord who?

They started talking to me about someone named Jesus. They began to tell me that this man died two thousand years ago for my sin. They told me he sent them there that I might be born again. "Well, what's that?" I said. Then they started telling me he wants me. All I need to do was pray with them and that Jesus would come in my heart. They began to tell me how he loved me and he knew where I would be that night and what I had on my mind.

That night I was looking up through the bottom, Jesus knew I was on my way out. I asked the Lord into my heart that night, and I cried and cried. I felt love like I had never felt love before.

Then get this, the phone rang. And it's one of the oldest sisters of mine, and I answered the phone. I had not talked to her like forever, and she said to me, "Is Ruby there?"

I said, "Yes. I just got saved." She was the first one I confessed to that I was saved.

> If you confess with your mouth the Lord Jesus and believe in your heart that God raised Him from the dead, you will be saved. For with the heart one believes unto righteousness, and with the mouth confession is made unto salvation. (Romans 10:9–10, NKJV)

It came right out of me. What came out of my mouth was, "Hey, I just got saved, not the Scripture." When I woke up the next morning, I got a call from my significant other. She was pretty upset, and I went back there. You know, nobody told me to read the Bible, go to church, or get baptized; they told me nothing. But when I went back to what was my home and family, I noticed a new loving voice that I had never heard before—and it was the sweetest, most loving, most gentle voice I had ever heard. When I was doing something that was not good, I would hear him say to me, "You know that's not good for you." That was it. No, that's it! I am done with you, not the hammer is coming down, nothing of that sort.

The Holy Spirit was in me, and I did not know it. I took him to places you ought not to take him, but I did not knowing anything. I found myself roll over in bed every night and tell the Lord I was sorry. I did not know anything about repenting or about 1 John 1–9 (NKJV) that says, "If we confess our sins, He is faithful and just to forgive us our sins and cleanse us from all unrighteousness."

Confession keeps your fellowship with God, and I found out that it does not matter how many times you fall. It only matters that you get up one more time than you fall. You know, this went on for about a year—whether it was sex, dope, or drinking. He talked to me at other times too. I was riding around in Green Bay looking for a place. I was going to fill out an application at, and I was kind of lost, and I heard that new voice inside of me helping me and showing me where to go. I thought that was so cool. It did not matter. He loved me out of everything. I was lost as a puppy, and he just kept coming after me.

Day after day, I even tried to make deals with him because this was my family, and it was wrong in his sight. The homosexuality was wrong, not the love. I would pray in my head and say, *God, I will stop drinking, swearing,* all that I thought was bad. But I did not want to give up the lifestyle, and not smoking dope meant I had to like not walk in the fog.

I said, "God, I will quit dope," and I smoked it some days nonstop most of the day: breakfast, lunch, and dinner. Before and after if I had it. Well, needless to say, he is not into deals. He wants all of you, and he wants it the right way according to his Word. You know, people who have to stay drunk or stoned, whatever your vice may be, you are just someone who is hurting inside; and that's the only way to stop the pain even if it's just for a few hours or days or all our lives. It helps to numb us, so we can get through another day and not deal with abuse.

You know, someone who has been sexually abused, whether it happened once or the first eighteen years of your life, sexual abuse is not just sexual. It is mental, physical, emotional, and spiritual abuse. It takes so much of a child, and people do it every day and just walk away as if nothing happened, and that child is devastated! A child takes years to process what has happened to them. And people will say stuff like, "Why did not they tell their mom?" Well, because they don't know how to say it or know what happened to them. You know, when I asked the Lord into my heart, it was as if I was blind, and now I could see. I could do anything I wanted and did not have any remorse about it. I did not feel bad about it or guilty, and believe it or not, I just could not see anything wrong with how I lived; but I hated the hiding and the secret junk that went with it 'cause society frowned on homosexuality.

Now I had asked the Lord into my heart, and I would have sex and could see the wrongness of it. I would ask for forgiveness every night. I had not told Lee what I had done. I needed to be ready to go when I did. I did not want her to know that this battle went on in me for quite a while. It was like I had the Devil on one side telling me to stay and God on the other side loving me and telling me, "You don't want to stay here and live like this." Now to most people who do not understand homosexuality I was scum 'cause we all know sin is something I do that you don't. Anyway, God loved me out of one thing at a time. I remember the day I drove out of the town we lived in.

As I drove out, there was this stretch of road about a mile long that was a two-lane highway with nothing but trees on both sides, and as I got to the end of that stretch of road, I looked up. And the sun was shining through the clouds. I saw beams of light shining through. I had never saw that before. It was the most beautiful thing I had ever seen in my whole twenty years.

And somehow I just knew: God was smiling at me that day. I had chosen him. That's what he wants. He has given us a choice. God gave us a choice. He gave us a choice of life and good or death and evil (Deuteronomy 30:15). That is what he wants. He wants to be chosen by us, not force us to choose him. Who have you decided to make your god?

CHAPTER 2

Childhood

Judy Lyn Zotos was born June 15, 1960, to Harry and Glenda Zotos. We lived in Stickney, Illinois. My parents rented a building where they ran a bar called the Stickney Liquors; it was their business. When I was about one and a half, they bought a tavern, and my dad named it the Red Heads Lounge; he named it after my mom. Believe it or not, my earliest memory is when I was still in my crib; the end of my sister Jackie's bed met the side of my crib. I climbed out one night, landed on her bed, and went over and sat on her head with a wet diaper. Jackie was not happy when I showed up 'cause she was not the baby anymore. I was told this when I grew up, so I must have been ticked at her. She probably teased me or something when I was in my crib. Anyway, I had been told when I was a baby, I was the best baby my mom ever had 'til I started to walk or got out of the crib. All they would say is, "Judy would lay in her crib and play with her feet." They said the only time they would hear from me was when I was hungry or wet, and all they had to do was prop a bottle up for me in my crib or change my diaper and I was fine.

This was said by my older siblings; they range in ages twelve to twenty years older than me; this does not include Jackie. She is only three years older than me. To me, this explained why when I got to be a teen, I needed touching 'cause I never had it. I had a woman tell me at church one day that her mom thought she held her baby too much. I told her what I just told you, and I told her if she did not hold her son enough, someone else would, and it probably would not be a healthy thing. Make sure he is whole and nurture him. I do believe it is a part of a healthy emotional building of a child. As a child, I pretty much took care of myself. I really don't remember a lot of anyone really being there at all. My mom worked nights when I was very young at a restaurant nights for a while, and my dad tended our tavern. When I was around three years, old my mom started sleeping in the back apartment.

You see, we owned the building, and the bar was on the main floor; and we lived upstairs. There were two bedrooms and a kitchen and living room in the front apartment, and the back was a small one bedroom with a kitchen and living room, and the backdoor went down to the main floor where you could either go into the bar or outside into the yard, so it had its own entrance and so did the one in the front; it went out into the sidewalk out front which was a very busy street called Harlem Avenue. I was told that my dad brought my mom's first five children up here and put them in school, bought them clothes, and took care of them. But I have been told that the oldest came up before my mom and dad started dating. My dad was not a bad man; he just had a problem with alcohol. Now having all these people around Jackie and I, you would think that we would have been well taken care of, wouldn't you? I remember being in my diaper and playing in the closet with matches. My dad would leave his cigarettes on the coffee table in the living room with his matches, so I know where I got them. I took them in the closet and set the floor on fire, or at least that's what I remember burning. And when I got older, that floor was black where I had burned it. I remember the door flying open, and it was my mom; she pulled me out and spanked me pretty good after she put the fire out. She always used a switch off a tree, so it hurts.

I remember we had this very long staircase that went out the front door of the front apartment. I went out the front door. I could not have been more than three years old. I remember falling down the stairs and walking back up, and I remember doing this over and over and over 'til I could walk up and down those stairs. I was always a very determined kid. I did the same thing with learning how to ride a two-wheeler. I took Jackie's two-wheeler when I was about five and just kept riding it 'til I got it. I would ride and fall then get back on and ride and fall; I did that 'til I got it. No one was there; I had no one to teach me, and since most of the time no one was watching me, I just did what I wanted. When I was about four, I had been told my mom looked outside early in the morning, and she saw me walking home in my pajamas and a coat not buttoned, eating a Drumstick ice cream cone I had gotten from the Dumpling House down the block. I would get money out of the cash register in our tavern and go get stuff. We lived in this place at 4207 South Harlem 'til I was about in second grade.

When I went in to school, I would walk; it was about eight blocks to school. I dressed myself, combed my hair stuff, and like that. There was a lady. I will call her Mrs. Sisters. She told me that when I was about fifteen years old when I was a little girl, she would watch me go to school, and she always knew no one was taking care of me 'cause she said I would wear shorts in the winter and long pants in the summer. She told me she would follow me to and from school and make sure I got there and got home. I used to have the older girls like Jackie's age; they would make fun of me because I had too much VO5 in my hair. That should paint the picture of the dirty little kid that I was.

When I was about six years old, my brother took Jackie and I to a place called Cermak Pool and threw us off the high dive in about eight feet deep of water and told us to swim, and we did. He had some friends who let him in with us before the pool opened at 10:00 a.m., so no one else was in the pool. I started riding my Stingray there every time I could. I would stay there from the time it opened 'til it almost closed. I would get out and go to the food stand and get a hot dog and then go back and swim. It cost a dime for kids to get in and swim. I rode my Stingray across Harlem Ave. through the path in the woods over the bridge on Ogden and to the pool. Sometimes my mom would come looking for me outside the fence. I was always supposed to be home before dark. Sometimes I would forget. My dad would walk there sometimes and drink beer and fish in the pond there; that was our family outing. I don't remember anyone ever hugging me or giving me birthday parties or anything a family does. I remember watching my friends go home for dinner and always wishing I had to, but I never had to. When I got hungry, I would go home and eat whether it was cereal or a bag of chips and a coke from our tavern; it did not matter. No one seemed to tell me that stuff. When I was about two years old, I ran out into Harlem Ave. I remember looking to my right and seeing a very big red truck coming at me, and someone grabbed me and threw me front ways into the woods that were across the street from our bar. All I remember is someone in a white suit of some sort carried me up the stairs and gave me to my dad who was sleeping and told him to watch me.

When I was a baby (I don't know how old I was probably about three), one of my older sisters who was only fifteen was taking Jackie to school in my mom's car, and either before or after the school, she was driving down Pershing in Stickney. Cars were beeping at her, and people were yelling at her and pointing at the back of the car; and when she looked, she saw me hanging on the back inside of the door, and the door was wide open. She pulled over and put me back in the car. Some stuff are probably good not to remember. I was told that story. Apparently, getting to age eight was a miracle for me.

CHAPTER 3

Adolescence

When I was about 4.5 years old, I remember Jackie had some kind of a book that she had to read, and I was trying to help her or something. I know I was not in school yet, and I remember a picture that was taken of us then, and I saw in the picture that Bob was there, and he put his hand on my shoulder in the picture. That's how I know I was about 4.5 when he started molesting me because that was what I was doing, reading with Jackie; and then when my mom was not there, he took me into my mom's bed and did things to me that I really did not understand. I remember he would put a pillow over me eyes and do stuff to me sexually, then he would say to me in a very scary tone, "You better not tell anyone about this." I did not tell; I just know my innocence was taken that first time, and I know the shame I felt and the filth I felt, and it would be years before that filthy, dirty feeling would leave. And if it was not for God, it never would have. Bob was eventually my stepdad and would molest me every chance he got. Leviticus 18:5–18 talks all about uncovering someone's nakedness. God did not ever want this in my life, but he could not stop what my parents had sown, but I am thankful that God looked down and said, "I will get my girl back." And he did, and he has been the one who put me back together, which is something no man could ever do. God is a lover, and I pray every one who reads this book will know him for who he really is and fall so deeply in love with him that you would never look anywhere else for wholeness and peace. He would never let you down; never!

My parents stopped sleeping together when I was very young, around three; they got a divorce when I was about seven or eight years old. They sold the bar right around then which would have been around 1968.

Jackie and I were told we had to go with my mom, and we got apartment in Summit, Illinois, and my mom's boyfriend Bob moved with us. Yes, the same pedophile that molested me to start with. He came into our room one night, looking under our covers; and Jackie told my mom the next day. And when my mom asked him about it, he told her he was looking for his keys, and she believed him. Jackie and my mom got into a big argument, and Jackie moved out. She went to live with a couple of my sisters, one at a time, of course. But I had to stay, and my mom who worked nights, left me at home with Bob when he was home. I really missed Jackie. I was more vulnerable than before, but it was not Jackie's fault. She tried to stop it, but she just got hurt trying to stop it. See, he had already started on me when we had the bar, but what does a four-and-a-half-year-old girl know about what someone they trust and love is doing to them? And then they tell you to never tell anyone and scare the crap out of you. That went on for a couple of years. He got to get me by myself any chance he got, then we moved to Cicero, Illinois. My mom, Bob, and I.

I was still in third grade, and Mom was not there some-times at night. Bob would come into my bedroom at night when Mom was not there. I was being abused sexually, mentally, physically, emotionally, and spiritually. Pedophiles take everything away from you, and a child does not even know they are being taken from until one day when you are a teen, you can see what was being done; and it hurts so bad 'cause you trusted this monster and even looked up to them, and you'd realize what they were doing the whole time. And then it's one of the toughest things you ever face because a child has no idea of what is going on, and as a child, you know something is not right. And you feel dirty and ashamed, but you think it's your fault, and they let you think that.

Well, one night I am not sure of what time it was, but it was late; and I don't think my mom was home. Bob came into my room and exposed himself, and I remember looking at him and just saying no and that I did not want him in there, and he pulled his pants back up and walked out of the room. Then the trouble started with him. He did weird stuff like try to get my mom mad at me like telling her I lied about brushing my teeth and saying I had not taken a bath when I had and started telling me I was stupid and stuff like that.

You see, if I was doing what he wanted, I could have whatever I wanted, and I mean anything. I was the best thing since homemade apple pie, but when I said no to him, he hated me and would try to make my life as miserable as he could, and he did to. I started stealing a lot from stores and people after that. I would walk into the drug store and walk out with cases of Pepsi and, for some reason, tennis balls and tennis rackets. He still did stuff after I said no to him; it was not as often. I think that was because we had moved to Romeoville back where his own home was, and his ex-wife lived at the end of the block with some friends of hers and my stepdad's daughter. He had more access to her now, so he did not molest me as much. I did find out later he had been molesting her also; she was a sweet kid. She was killed by a drunk driver when she was eighteen years old. She was six months pregnant with her boyfriend's child who was driving the truck when they were hit head on by a drunk driver, and the baby was pushed into her chest. She never knew what hit her.

Bob went into a deep depression after that and actually tried to blame my mom for his daughter's death. He said it was because my mom would not let Sandy come live with them. I was told by my mom that his daughter did not want to live with him, and now my mom knows why. His sons lived with him, so he did not have as much privacy to molest me as he did when it was just him, Mom, and I. He did take advantage of times when nobody was around though until I was about eleven years old. He would try to get me to drink booze and get me drunk on holidays and stuff. He was a very sick man. Now I do believe he was demon-possessed. It was told to my mom by his father that he had been booted out of the Marine Corps after he was only in there for about three months. It was a general discharge. I had been told no one could find the papers as to why, and they were sealed by the Marines, so only God knows why.

You know, when I was a child, I did not have a whole lot of guidance. I did not know that an adult could be such a monster. I looked up to this man, thinking he really cared about me because he was the only adult that ever took real time with me. I trusted him with all of me. I had no idea he was taking my everything away. He took my childhood, my womanhood, my innocence, and my trust in people. It hurts so bad when I found out what was really going on, and this whole thing would change my life for years; and to most people, it cripples for life—emotionally, mentally, physically, and sexually. Emotionally, your relationships are not what they ever could be because you are hiding so much, and you are taking so much out on the innocent people who just want to have a life with you. But the so-called baggage can get into the relationships, and you don't even know it. All you know is, there are things about this person who remind you of the people who hurt you, and you can always find something wrong in anyone when you are looking for it. Mentally, you don't think correct most of the time. You think everyone wants to have sex with you if they show any interest in you or any attention they pay toward you. I believe this because you thought the person who did the molesting really cared; and it twists or perverts or clouds your thinking about people.

Physically, I did everything I could to make sure no man took any interest in me. I ate to feed that thing in me that needed comfort, and I just got bigger and bigger. I dressed in clothes that were way too big and sloppy. I did not want any attention that most women like from men. When I first got saved about twenty-five years ago, I had someone tell me I ate food because I was in fear of any man ever taking interest in me. I did not ever want to be molested again, so that was what I did to not get any attention from men. I was told the same thing about twenty years later, then I realized they were right. Sexually, sins of the parents open doors for Satan to come in and do things to their children at a very young age.

I knew something was very wrong. I remember being about six years old and sitting up in a crab apple tree we had in our backyard at our tavern. While I was sitting there, a really nice car pulled up in our parking lot. It was a black Lincoln. I did not know that then, but I do know that now. Anyway, a man got out of the driver's side. He was wearing a suit and tie. He walked over to the passenger side and opened the door for a very pretty woman who was wearing a dress and a mink stole around her shoulders. I remember whistling at her, and then I grabbed my mouth with my hand and thought, *I was not supposed to do that. I am a girl.* I knew then something was wrong right there.

CHAPTER 4

Teenager

When I was about eleven years old, Jackie and I told my dad what Bob had been doing, and he handed Jackie a blank check and told her to get us an apartment. He still lived in Stickney, so the next time Jackie and I came out to be with him for the weekend, we got a paper and went and found one at 4127 S. Harlem Ave. It was a block from where our tavern was. We told my mom we were moving with my dad, and to my surprise, she let me go; and Jackie was living with my sister Nikki, so she could go. Nikki was my sister from my dad's first marriage. Jackie and Nikki got along real well. I was glad Jackie could live with Nikki because Nikki had a house with her family about two blocks from my stepdad's house where I lived with my mom and him. But now Jackie and I were back together, and I was so happy about that. Jackie always tried so hard to take care of me, and that was a tough job, but she was a tough chick. One thing I always knew, Jackie loved me no matter what I did. We would fight like normal sisters, but no one else could ever touch either one of us without answering to the other. We moved in, and we got furniture. Jackie made our house a home the best she could.

My dad got up about 5:00 a.m. to go to work. He did not drive ever that I know of, so he had to catch a bus about 5:30 a.m. and go somewhere where some friends he worked with would pick him up and drive him the rest of the way. He was gone about eleven hours a day from Monday through Friday. He would walk to the bar about a block from our house and have a beer or two, then he would walk to the Jewel on the corner and buy something for dinner and come home and cook it. My dad was the best cook I have ever known. He could be blind staggering drunk and come home and cook a dinner that you would have thought he cooked all day.

My dad was a good man; he just had a problem with drinking. I believe his childhood had no love in it. He could never tell you he loved you. His way of telling you he loved you was to hand you money and tell you to go buy something for yourself. He tried very hard to take good care of Jackie and me, but I guess it was too late as far as the damage that was already done to me.

From the time Jackie and I moved with my dad until he died, he did everything he knew to take care of us, and he always kept a roof over our heads, gave what we needed to live, and bought us most everything we wanted. That was the way he knew to take care of us. My dad was ten years older than my mom, so when I was eleven and we moved with him, he was fifty-five years old. As I look at it, I realize he had some long days, but he did it to take care of us. You know, when I was with my mom, he always paid his child support. He never missed. When Jackie and I were not with him, he lived in a room with a TV and a bed and a dresser by himself. I used to feel bad when we would go see him for the weekend, and we would have to leave him there by himself. I never liked leaving him.

Well, we lived on the second floor, and the girl downstairs introduced me to pot. So I started getting high and smoking cigarettes. I dressed like a guy already, and I hated school. I think everyone just thought I would grow out of the tomboy thing, but that was not what the deal was. I was a homosexual, and I never did anything about it. I wanted to but did not know how to tell anyone about it, and I did not meet anyone who was also homosexual until I was sixteen years old.

Jackie and I were on our own still. We were used to that, and my dad had to work. A lot of the responsibility for me was put on Jackie. She always had that Mommy thing going on, and she did the best she could. When I say we were on our own, what I mean is, we really did not have much guidance. We always had a roof over our heads and always had food on the table, and we had love, kind of, because we did have the bare necessities that we needed to live. But we did not have the family thing, you know, where you have dinner together and someone tucks you in at night or someone there to tell you how to dress that day or what to eat for breakfast or all the things I believe parents would guide you in. I know when we moved with my dad, he was gone at least eleven hours a day, and I really had to get up for school on my own and did everything on my own. Most of the time, Jackie would help me, but if I got in trouble for not going to school, I remember my dad calling from work and making sure I was up. I don't think he really knew what to do with me sometimes. I was as rebellious a kid could be who had been molested most of her childhood.

He never spanked Jackie or me. Mom did that, and I am thankful for that now. Of course I was not then, but now I am glad she did because if she hadn't, I would have been worse, if that's possible. It seems like when you live in apartments or at least the ones I always lived in, there were so many people you just got to know. When we lived in the first apartment we rented, I met a girl that was my age. She had four other kids in her family. She was the oldest. I started hanging around with them a lot. I would go over there, and we would sneak her mom's cigarettes and go upstairs in her room and smoke, or they had a door up there; we could go out and smoke on the roof. We would do a lot of stuff up there. I don't ever remember her mom coming up there. Her mom was divorced. She was raising her children with no input from a dad at all. I never met him or saw him. Then I figured out some stuff; her mom was a lesbian, and the place they lived at was the back of a tavern; that's why the apartment was attached. The bar itself was a homosexual bar. You could never see in this place, but if my friend wanted to ask her mom something, we would go in there; and then if you just looked around, you could see what the deal was. But my friend never mentioned it, and neither did I. I knew something was up when we would come into her house early in the morning, and her mom's bedroom door would be locked; and a couple hours later, her mom and a lady friend of hers would come out. They usually looked like they had a rough night, and they had been in the bar all night. My friend's mom was good friends with the owner of the bar. We were friends until I was about thirteen, and I am not real sure, but I think when my friend had fallen and cut her face real bad on a pipe at a construction site, her mom did not want her hanging out with me. It was not my fault she fell, but I guess her mom thought it was.

I had gotten to know some neighbors who were older than I was; they were married and had kids. They partied hard. I started to drink a lot there and smoke a lot of dope. Their younger sister was only a couple years older than I was; she was Jackie's age. I remember this guy Bob. He was this lady's husband. He had a lot of biker friends that would come over to the house, and we would party a lot. So I was about thirteen, and I was into a lot of stuff I should not have been. These people had some serious drugs, and there was not anything I would not take, and they had it all. They had Reds, 714 Quaaludes, Black Mollies, Yellows, Acid, Mesk, and LSD. Anyway, you get the picture. If you wanted up or down and trails whatever you wanted, I would get pretty stoned. Then I would take stuff home for Jackie and her boyfriend whom she would later marry. And they would get pretty stoned. I could bring stuff home because on Friday and Saturday night, my dad was usually at the bar medicating himself too. Pain inside of us is why we drink or do dope or whatever your pleasure is—whether it's the drunk or the stoner you are still trying to get numb, and I don't care who you are; it's the truth.

Problem is, when you wake up, the pain is right there. And yes, you escaped for a short time, but it's all right back in the morning or when the stuff wears off. I could never get drunk enough or high enough. I drank and smoked and did more drugs than anybody around me, and that included guys too. And never thought I was high or drunk, figure that one. I met some people who were way older than I was about twelve, and they were in their thirties when I met them. They were married, and she was an alcoholic, and he just seemed to work a lot. She did not have any kid. Her name was Mary, and his was Dave. They were like a set of parents for me because Mary always told people I was her adopted daughter, and she treated me as I was just that. She would cook me breakfast, and if I wanted to stay for dinner, Dave would cook really good dinners. I always felt so loved there even though they were as messed up as I was.

I don't know why they were good to me. I would cut school, and Mary would call in for me, and I would stay at her house all day. They lived in this place Dave called the Chicken Coop. It was a small two-room apartment, if you could call it that, with a half bath; and if they wanted a shower, they had to go to the shower building next to it. It sounds really tacky, but I always felt safe there until Dave would have enough of Mary's mouth and beat the crap out of her. She always got him pretty mad about every three months saying all kinds of stuff like the house was hers and the cars were hers and just stuff to aggravate him, and I would tell her to stop. But she just got worse, and he would hit her pretty bad, and she would be like a lamb for a while; then she would start. And you knew it was coming. You just did not know when the bomb was going to go off.

Dave would teach me how to fix cars. I would go outside while he was working on his car, and I always liked working on cars, so he would show me stuff. He taught me how to tune my cars up and change belts. I got to where I could change radiators. I could just always fix mostly anything. I took a lot of stuff apart when I was very young. I took apart my dad's radios, tape recorders, phones, and whatever else I could get my hands on. Some, I could put back together; and some, I got bored with, so I just left them in pieces.

When I was about fourteen years old, I started hanging out with someone. I knew as a very young child, and we started going to the woods. Now we would get people to buy us beer and have smoke, and we would go there and see who could drink the most and get the highest, and I usually won that one. Of course, I had more than one time when one of my best friends at the time (his name was John) would come up to me and say, "Judy, what are you doing laying in the river?"

And I would say, "John, I am not laying in the river." See, I would have been at the edge of the water and just pass out and not even know it; and John, being the great friend he was, would help me out of there and help me walk. I had that happen more than once. You know, God, for some reason, was watching me even then 'cause there were a lot of weird people in those woods, probably including me. But some of these people would rape chicks and really hurt people, but even then, there was a biker. His name was Russ. He would watch out for us young girls, and he would not let these guys touch us. I remember one time in particular that a guy was trying to get me to go with him in his car. I remember his name even, but Russ stepped in and made this guy back off. This guy was going to hurt me, and I was pretty scared, and it took a lot to get me afraid of anything, and I think Russ knew it. Now if you ever saw the arms on Russ, you would have listened to him. He took care of me that night, and he did not want anything for it. He just wanted to make sure no one would hurt me.

You know, God is so good. I do believe with all my heart that because of my mom's parents whom I found out later were Pentecostal preachers, I think God knew who I was. I only met my grandpa once. And then when he was dying in the hospital, I took my mom to see him. I do believe he waited for my mom to get there before he died because he died two hours after my mom saw him, and it took us twelve hours to drive to Meridian, Mississippi, which is where my mom is from. Her mother died of cancer at age thirty-nine. They did not believe in medicine, and she thought if God wanted her healed, she would be. So God blessed her anyway; she just did not have the faith. God has been very kind to me, and I am sure it's not for any other reason than it's because of who he is. It is one thing to love, but when you are love, that's something to really comprehend.

CHAPTER 5

My Dad

When I was fifteen, my dad was having a hard time with his lungs, and he went to the VA hospital for a checkup; and they did not take his voice box out, but they decided to put a hole in his throat to get the mucus out of his lungs, or at least that's what I was told. I remember going to the hospital with him and waiting for him to come out of surgery. Nikki, Jackie, and I were there; and when he came out of surgery, they wheeled him to a room, and we were waiting for him in a small area on the cancer floor. That should have been my first clue, but it was not. We did get to take him home soon after that. The day they put that hole in his throat was the day I never saw him smoke a cigarette again; he had to keep this thing cleaned out, and they gave him medicine of some kind. And I thought that was it and that he would be fine. Then all of a sudden, he has to go in for some kind of radiation, and I had no idea what was going on. I just kept living like a rebellious kid. When this happened, we had already moved down the block to 4029 S. Harlem Ave., still in Stickney, Illinois.

Jackie got married, and she lived a couple of blocks away, so it was just me and Dad. I had met some people in the building next to us. They were married and had a baby; he was about one year old. They were stoners too. I almost lived there. They were cool. I guess I did not realize what I was doing, and being fifteen, I was not really thinking any one cared. I just did whatever I wanted to. I would cut school and go to their house in the morning. By now I have tried to quit school, so they put me in this class at Morton East in Cicero where they put kids who won't go to school, and the mentally handicapped bus picked us up, and I probably belonged on that bus more than most people realized. But because I was only fifteen, I could not quit yet. So they made me go to this class. We had a teacher who was a hippie but one of those dignified ones with a degree; you know what I mean.

There were only about ten of us in this class. I knew some of these kids. We only had to stay a couple of hours a day, and I don't even remember doing anything like school. I think they were babysitting us until we could quit, but eventually, I stopped going to it anyway. There were some people I started hanging around with that did tic, angel dust, a lot of acid, and stuff like that. So I stayed out a lot, and my dad would walk the streets looking for me. Then after not finding me for a day or two, he would call Jackie and tell her he could not find the bum or SOB, which was his pet name for me. I get all warm when I hear that term. He used to tell me I was a bum and I would always be a bum. I am thankful God did not let that happen. My dad just did not know what to do, and he was dealing with his family curses or demons however you might want to say that. I never met any of my dad's family. He was from Greece, a small town right outside of Athens. I hope to go there some time. I had a family picture that he had. I cut him out of it. He looked like he was about eighteen in it. I cut him out because the rest of these people looked really depressed, and some looked angry. My dad was the best-looking one in there, but he was not smiling either. I don't think they were very happy people. I don't believe they knew love.

Well then, my dad went into the hospital after about one and a half year of dealing with this sickness that I found out later was really cancer, and I stayed in the apartment by myself. I was sixteen and a half at that time. Little did I know that was the last time I would see my dad at home. I went to the hospital to see him a lot. I just thought he would come home again. While he was gone, I had a lot of parties with friends and some people who I did not even know; we would drink quite a bit and do a lot of drugs. I was scared to be there by myself, so I would have parties and drink 'til I passed out most of the time. Some of my older friends would stay all weekend, but I would be alone when everyone went home, so I would go to sleep on the couch with a butcher knife under my pillow. I did not know what else to do. I guess I could have gone to Jackie's, but I did not. She had only been married about two years by now. Maybe I did not want to bother her and her husband. I don't really know. Maybe I did not want to tell anyone I was afraid. I really don't remember that one. Then after a couple of months of that, my sister Nikki called Jackie and asked her if I could come live with her. She saw to it that Jackie got some extra money from my dad dying, and Jackie put it down on a house eventually. In the meantime, she got an apartment in Berwyn with a bedroom for me, and I was happy about that probably more than she knew.

I was about sixteen and a half when I moved in with them; it was nice. I liked it, and Jackie never made me feel like I was just a visitor or I had to leave in a month. She and her husband were good to me. I got pretty close to Pat. Also, we were closer than I had ever been to my brother, for obvious reasons.

My mom gave me an insurance policy she had gotten when I was a baby, and I cashed it in and bought my first car. It was five hundred dollars. I bought a 69 Plymouth Fury; this thing was a boat. I used to drive it around the block 'til I got my Driver's license. Then I went to driving school and got my license.

After I was with Jackie for a couple of months, one morning on March 5, 1977, the phone rang at about five in the morning; and it was my sister Nikki. She called to tell us that my dad had died that morning. Jackie and I hugged and cried for a while. I remember how it hurt. I could not believe the pain and the hole in the middle of my being. I never knew something could hurt so badly. I loved my dad, but I knew I was not going to see him again. The last time I saw him, he looked at me, and he did not know me. Now he had already not known the others, but when he did not know me, I knew that was it. You see, I lived with him. I went to the hospital with him in the ambulance. The last time, he was home and he knew me. It was one of the hardest things I have ever done in my life, watching my dad suffer like that; but he never complained. He just laid in that hospital bed, and you could see the pain in his eyes, but he never said anything about it. He would just ask us to rub his back. He never said much after going in the hospital the last time.

You know, one time, I guess you could say I robbed a gas station while the people were right there. I was talking to the guys in the station, but they would wait on cars and then come back in. So they were in and out the whole time, and I knew where the key was to open the floor safe. I took it while they were out, and then I waited for them to come in and go back out, and I opened it and took this money bag out and stuck it in my coat. I put the key back and then left. I was only about thirteen or fourteen at the time. I went home and told Jackie what I did, and we counted the money. There was about six hundred dollars and a lot of change. So we went to the plaza and bought my dad this real nice leather recliner, and we tried to take it on the bus; but the driver would not let us. So we had to call a cab. We got it home and gave it to my dad, and I don't know what we told him, but he loved that recliner. Whenever he was home, he always sat in it. He always watched the Cubs game in it, and he liked Hamm's beer, so he would drink that and watch the game when he was home. My dad always liked what Jackie and I bought him. If it was clothes, he would wear them a lot. Now I don't blame him for anything. I understand now so much more than I did then. And, no, I did not get caught, and the station is no longer there.

You know, if my dad were here today, I would give him the biggest hug I could, and I would tell him how much I love him. And even if he did not receive Jesus, I would give him Jesus; and I do believe after he saw what Jesus has done in his daughter, he would happily receive the Lord of lords.

CHAPTER 6

Homosexual Living

I met some people when I was about sixteen years old. They were my age; they were friends with someone I knew when I was about five years old. It turned out she was homosexual too. She was seeing a girl, and I got to know these people pretty well; and I started seeing this girl when she broke up with my friend. I was kind of gun shy 'cause I did not really ever have a relationship with any one before, but she showed me some stuff. And I got in to the lifestyle pretty easily. I did not know anything else, and I did not feel anything else. I saw myself as very masculine, and if you can imagine being a woman and having feelings like a guy, you see, no matter what, it is not a good thing. People who live in this type of lifestyle mostly don't have a choice, and whether you are born that way or it is someone who is demon-possessed, it is still no life 'cause God said *no*! Leviticus 18:21 says that man shall not lie with man like he does with woman for this is an abomination unto God which, simply put, means it makes God want to puke, hurl, or hang noodles, whichever you prefer. You get the picture, right? I had enough lovers and thought I was in love with all of them and them to me, but it was nothing but straight-up lust, and my flesh was happy about it. The first person I was with taught me a lot about some stuff, but I still was not what I would call happy. I mean, I was happy like everyone else who was getting stoned and having sex most of the time. I had gotten a 1971 sunflower yellow Monte Carlo with a black vinyl roof and black lace interior; this car was nothing but Cherry dual exhaust and easy to work on 350 8 cylinder. I thought for sure this would fill that giant empty hole in me.

I had people stop me at red lights and tell me how sweet this car was, and it was. But you know, I still was not happy. I had someone who I loved very much, or at least I thought it was love for me. I thought it was love all the time. I had this nice car. I was young and pretty tough dressed, very butch. I was not comfortable any other way. I had people try to get me to dress what you would call feminine, and I felt like a true queer. It just did not work. I wanted to fit in but just never did—at least not with what you call normal women. So you go to people whom you have no secrets from. That's where you identify with these guys or girls. I felt very happy around other homosexuals or people who knew I was, and they accepted me. You know, Romans 1:32 (AMPC) says: "Though they are fully aware of God's righteous decree that those who do such things deserve to die, they not only do them themselves but approve and applaud others who practice them."

When I read that Scripture the first time, I understood it way too well; it is the truth. Anyone I knew who was homosexual was exactly like that 'cause most of us would have either lived in another state than our families for fear of rejection, or we just stayed away from family and other homosexuals and people who accept you. These people become your family. One of the biggest things at the bar was if somebody's mom would come to the bar. 'Cause most parents had rejected them and the pain of that is hard enough, let alone having nobody, so other people who understand try real hard to pick up the slack and love you, and that might not be something most could handle. But at least these people did not make you feel like a freak, so that's where you would go. But to those that accept you and try to be there for you, now I don't approve of it, but when I was in the middle of it, I could not see the problem with it 'cause it came as easy to me as breathing. It was not something I asked for one day or thought about becoming.

It chose me, and it is a life I don't believe anyone in their right mind would ever choose. It is empty, and it is dark; there is no life that I know of that is so empty. There is no future there. Most have no children; most have no one to grow old with 'cause the sin of sex out of marriage will eventually kill you, and it's not even God's judgment. You will reap what you sow. I don't care if you are straight as an arrow. If you are having sex out of marriage, it will kill you or any type of sin, but it does seem like sexual sin kills more people; and I believe that is 'cause it is a sin against your own body. We just don't realize how real Satan is, and when we get into sexual sin, we leave the door wide open for him to come in and destroy our lives. Now I personally did not know anything about God. I did not know about Jesus or what he had done for me. I had no idea who Jesus was, not a clue! And the funny thing is, there was a friend of mine whose mother was supposedly a Baptist, but she wanted to have sex with me. She asked her daughter to ask me if I would go out with her. I was seventeen, and her mother was, well, let's just say much older and keep it nice.

Anyway, my friend was drunk one night and started trying to tell me about Jesus, and I pretty much told her to shut up and leave me alone about it, and she did. It's funny when we don't know God or even think about him. We have no idea what is going on in us, and I saw nothing wrong with what I did or how I felt. I just thought this is what the deal is, and I thought I was born that way, and I saw nothing wrong with anything I did. I guess I was just straight-up godless like most. Well, I met someone when I was seventeen and a half. She was twenty years older than I was, but I really did not care; and she looked great. She did not look at all like she was thirty-seven. She had five kids. Her oldest was my age, and that kind of blew my mind; but I really did not give it a lot of thought at first. But after about a year, I did; and it did start to bother me.

Her two youngest were boys. I will call them William and Steve. They were three and six years old, and I loved them a lot. The youngest stole my heart though. He decided I was his, and I pretty much decided the same thing. He was mine. I spent a lot of time with him. He always wanted to be with me. If I was outside working on the car, he would come out there and play around me. He was happy as long as he was with me. If I went to the store, he went with me. Wherever I went, he wanted to go. I would get up on Saturday and Sunday with him, and we would play Legos together, or I would read to him. One of his favorite books was *The Count* who loves to count from Sesame Street. I taught him so much. I taught him how to count, to swim, and to ride a two-wheeler. He was my kid, if I ever had one.

You see, his dad died of a massive heart attack at age thirty-three. He thought he was a healthy guy. There was no reason he should have died. He was not over weight or anything, but he was an over-the-road truck driver; and back then, they could call you back out after you were only home for eight hours. And Lee told me that night when he left, she looked into his eyes when he was leaving. And she said his eyes were bloodred. She asked him not to go, but he said he had to. He died of a massive heart attack on that trip on the Pennsylvania Turnpike. He lived long enough to pull the 18-wheeler over, and he was gone. Well, Steve was only like two years old, but he was Daddy's boy; and he would not let Lee do anything for him. When his dad was home, he would only let him change him or feed him, and he only wanted his dad to take care of him. So when his dad died, he was lost. I did not know them at the time. I met them about a year later, and Steve was quite a lost little boy, but he just latched on to me, and I loved him very much too. It broke my heart the day I walked outside of our house in Wisconsin, and Steve was sitting on his tricycle at the end of the driveway; and when I walked over and asked him what he was doing, he said, "I am looking for Daddy." How do you explain to a three-year-old boy Daddy is never coming home? I know why he attached himself to me. It was 'cause he needed me big-time, and I probably needed him too. When I met Lee, she was bound and determined to take care of me, and I fell in love with her too.

When I met her, I lived in Cicero with Dave and Mary. Lee was Dave's sister figure that one. I met her at Dave's on Christmas of 1978. I never asked her if she knew about me. I can only guess that she did. And on New Year's Eve, things happened; and before I knew it, I was moving to Wisconsin and living with her in a beautiful house that she gave me after I was there about a week. Her daughter who was in high school lived with us, and Lee told her on the way home to Wisconsin that she was in a relationship with me, and she was not real happy about it. Lee told her if she did not like it and that she could live with her dad. Well, her daughter fell in love with me too. It took a little while, but we got along real good after a while. You know, it was a serious relationship, and I thought it was for life. It was everything I wanted—someone to love and kids and a house, a two-and-a-half car garage, and everything but the white picket fence. It was everything I wanted, and you know God will give you what you want even if it's wrong. He gave the Israelites a king when he wanted to be their king. God wants us to choose him, and if we don't, he will give you what you want because he is a gentleman, and he will not force himself on anyone. God showed me that everything I thought would fill that huge hole in the center of me just was not the answer. And believe me, I got everything I wanted. I was always blessed in getting everything I wanted no matter what. If I had to work for it, I did.

Somehow I always got what I wanted. I was always trying to shove something in that hole in the middle of me; and the next thing I wanted, I would do it. And I had relationships, drugs, cars, money, and places to live that were nice—an extremely nice home with big yard. I mean, I had it all by the time I was eighteen; it was handed to me. Here, you can have it. Just stay here and love me and take care of me and my kids. I did not even have to work if I did not want to. She had enough to take care of me and the kids financially, but I could not handle that fact of it being money from his death and stuff like that, so I got a job working in a wood-working plant. We made cabinets and, well, a lot of stuff. I drove a forklift or cut wood on saws or whatever they needed me to do. It was a guy's job, but I found it easy because that was how I saw myself. I lived there for two years, and I loved them. They were my family, but after I gave my heart to the Lord, I could not stay there because now I could see it for what it was. And Lee knew it, and it broke her heart and mine. I tried to make a lot of deals with God; but needless to say, he is not into deals. He wants your all. He wanted my heart, and he wanted theirs too. And later, Lee did give her heart to the Lord, but I don't know what happened with all of them 'cause I had to stay away; or I would fail because my heart would have went there for a while. Anyway, but then, I would have just gotten miserable again and had to leave again and put them through the pain again. When I left there, I left praying that if I did what God wanted me to, the Lord would take care of them, especially Steve. I probably thought about him more than anyone else because once again, this kid was being left.

CHAPTER 7

Going For God

When I left, I went to Jackie's and stayed there for a while 'til I got a job. I got a good job at a gear shop where they made bevel gears and pinions for oil rigs. It paid pretty good for 1981, so I got an apartment in Cicero and lived there for a small time because I got laid off after ten months. The unemployment rate was very high, and I could not find a job anywhere.

I ended up staying with my sister that had led me to the Lord for some time at least six months. I started going to church with her where I met a pastor at a Pentecostal church who—even though I was dressed like a guy wearing jeans, a flannel, and gym shoes—welcomed me with open arms. I remember the first time I met her. She gave me a hug and welcomed me and always treated me the same whenever I came to church. This was a nice church but not much Word being taught. It had a lot of praise and worship a lot of tongues and prophecy but not much Word. I liked going there for a while, but soon I realized it was not going to help me even though God was still loving me out of stuff, like after I had left Wisconsin, I still needed deliverance from homosexuality; but the Lord started dealing with me about other stuff like the music I was listening to. I would be driving my car and cranking Jethro Tull or Led or Janis, and the Lord would softly nudge me and just convict me because of where this music took me.

So a lot of times, whatever I was listening to would go flying out the window. Now I don't recommend that anyone else do that. It was just how I did some stuff. I did the same with cigarettes and reefer and other stuff. I would flush stuff and get to Jonesing for some cigs or reefer and go out and buy it. But eventually, I would get the victory. Somehow, I always repented and went on. I just knew if I did not quit, I was not going to make it. I have heard it said it's not how you start but how you finish. I just knew that God would not give up on me, and I am so thankful that he just never did.

I stayed with some other people for a small time and still could not get a job anywhere. It was like a wall was in front of me, and I just could not get a job. It did caused me to spend time reading my Bible and going to some prayer meetings. I remember being at a prayer meeting, and I wanted to raise my hands and praise God, but I felt funny or embarrassed. And I remember a lady at the meeting who was into prophecy. She looked over at me and said, "The Lord told me to tell you that you can raise your hands anywhere you want and worship him," and I was set free from that day on.

After that, I did not care who was around or anything 'cause I knew I had God's permission—and that was all I needed. Then I learned about fasting, and I came to live at my mom's house which was a drag because Bob was still here, and I did not like being under the same roof as him for obvious reasons. I was not free from the hate of him yet. As a matter of fact, I was planning his murder on some days. Anyway, I began to spend a lot of time reading my Bible and fasting, and I remember one day as I had been fasting for about five or seven days, at the end of that fast, I got a call from someone who I did not know. I was fasting and believing God for a job, and this person told me on the phone that the Lord told her to call me and tell me I had been faithful over little, and he was going to make me faithful over much. And in the next couple of weeks, I got a job working at a convalescent home, and it was not much; but it sure beat zero. And when I went to work there, it was like God just put a happier full of joy spirit in me, and those older people would hear me whistling while I was mopping the floors. And they would say, "Judy is here." And they just would get blessed, and after a while, I really enjoyed them; but the hours kind of were a drag and so was the pay. But after a while, I got a better job working at Rockwell International, and that was better pay and insurance and day shift with weekends off, and I did stay at the home for a while working weekends because I had gotten attached to the people there. All they wanted was a smile and a couple minutes of my time, and I got their time too. So it was a give and take.

I could not believe how a lot of those people who had kids would only come to see them about once or twice a year. I did not think there was any excuse for that, but I did try to make up for that with some of them the best I could, and one lady even knitted me some booties; she was a sweetheart.

I worked at Rockwell and went to church and read my Bible. By now I was free from some stuff—at least I thought I was until I got an apartment in Lockport and started smoking dope again, and I never did stop smoking yet. I was trying very hard to serve God, but I just was not getting free of some stuff yet. I was told they were habits, and I would get free anyway.

I did not start smoking dope again until someone laid some serious condemnation on me about some stuff, and I just walked out of their house, and I backslid for a long time. I was very hurt, and when I had went to another church, a prophecy came to me from a woman, and she said the Lord had seen what was done, and I was to stay away from that house where the person had hurt me and that the fall of that house was going to be great, and unfortunately, it was. But God got me back, and I was very thankful. When I was at Rockwell for a while, I met someone named Cheryl who became one of the best friends I would ever have. She was one of those solid people you know who pretty much was raised under almost normal circumstances. Even though when I met her I was away from the Lord, God got her saved one night while I was out. She was watching Jimmy Swaggart and gave her heart to the Lord. You know, Rev. Swaggart got more people saved in sin than a lot of people will ever in their Christianity.

Cheryl was raised Catholic, and I mean they really went to church and did the lent thing and stuff like that. I have heard it said it is a great place to come from, and that's good. At least she knew all about Jesus, and she did have a lot of faith; and then she got born again. And she began to read her Bible, and she loves the Lord a lot. Cheryl and I became best friends, and we still are. I am very thankful for her. She is one of those people who know how to listen and know when to say something and when not to. Sometimes we just need someone who will listen and just put their arm around us and let us cry it out. Cheryl has always been a rock for me; she is a very intelligent woman. I always tell her she is book smart and life dumb, and I don't mean that in a rude way. I guess no matter how you say that, it is not nice. But what I mean is, she knows a lot about stuff like books and school stuff I should have learned in school. But the stuff I learned out on the street dealing with people, she has not experienced, and that is good. She still has some innocence about her, and that is nice.

Cheryl and I worked at Rockwell for years, and then we shared an apartment for a while; and we ended up living together for about fourteen years. You know, Cheryl and my relationship started out wrong, but I am thankful it became right because I sure would have hated to lose her friendship, faithfulness, and her loyalty—and Cheryl is one of the most loyal people I have ever met. She would do anything for you. She is truly a friend that sticks closer than a brother, and when God gives you one of those, it is one gift that you cannot put a price on. Marilyn Hickey said, "If you have found one true and loyal friend, you are a blessed person." And I do agree because I have had plenty of people tell me they love me, but when the chips were down, the only one that came through was Cheryl every time.

Cheryl and I were invited to go to a church that a lady we worked with went to, so we went and visited there one time; and I walked out thinking, *I won't be back here again.* We went to this church. I think it was the pastor's wife's birthday, and there is this big window behind the pulpit; and the curtains were closed. And someone decided to open them when the pastor was talking, and there were two clowns out on a scaffold, and they were trying to put up a happy birthday sign, so they closed the curtain. And some other stuff happened, and I remember thinking, *I don't think so.*

Well, we left. And I told Cheryl that I did not think this was the place for us. So I went home, and for the next month, the Holy Spirit just kept nudging me about going back. And finally we went back, and I began to be taught the Word of God like I had never been taught before.

CHAPTER 8

The Word of God

I started going to a church called the House of Glory, which I thought was a pretty interesting name for a church. It's the one we had visited before with the clowns. Pastor Robb Thompson is the senior pastor there and still is. He had gotten born again in a mental institution. He had lost his mind and could not figure out who was really talking to him in his mind and ended up after about three months of no sleep and living in fear, he said he had at least seven conversations going on in his mind. So one night in the mental ward, a janitor asked him if he would go to heaven if he breathed his last breath that night, and he told him "yes." The janitor asked him *why*. He thought that, and he said because he was a good guy.

Then the janitor told him, "If being good could get you there, then why did Jesus have to go to the cross?" So he got saved that night, and he went to sleep holding a Bible. And he said he woke up a new man. He would only read the Word for months, and the Word helped him and gave a man with no mind back his mind.

Well, I started going to church faithfully. I go on Sunday morning and night and Wednesday evenings. I began to meditate on the Word like never before. One of the first things I was taught was that God loved me. That alone blew my mind to think of a God who loves me. Wow, I don't remember being told that at all. I always thought I was so bad. I thought how could God love me, and does God really love people? That's not the God I had always heard about. I heard he was always angry at us and that we were not good enough for him. It was a major change for me to even think he loves me. Man, that alone changed me some. Then I began to hear how we should read our Bibles every day, and don't get me wrong, I did read my Bible a lot before; but it was because the Holy Spirit would prompt me not to because anyone ever said it was for survival. I did not have any idea what I was about to learn. All I knew was, I have been saved for about six years, and I was not getting very far quick.

Yes, I had already stopped listening to a lot of serious rock and roll. I had a lot of convictions. I knew what was wrong now. At least after I got saved, I could see so much what I could not see before. I know my eyes were wide shut, if you know what I mean. I could party 'til I puked all day and all night and take all the drugs I wanted. Trust me, I took a lot. I could have sex when I wanted to and not feel bad a bit about it. I could steal. It just did not matter. I had no bad feeling about it. Well, maybe fear of getting caught doing some stuff. I ended up in jail more than once when I was sixteen. I had a 71 Monte Carlo; it was nice.

On Christmas Eve of 1978, I went to my mom's for dinner, had a few drinks, and then my stepbrother gave me a joint of Hawaiian for a present, so I saved it and went and picked up some friends. We went out and got some more booze and drank a lot more. I drank CC and Coke a lot, then we smoked the joint we had. We ended up picking up some other people, and we were pretty much just getting stoned then about one o'clock in the morning, I looked up. There were cops everywhere. Lights were flashing, and we were pulled over. There were about three or four police cars. I was asked to get out of the car, and I did. Then the cop asked for my driver's license, and I used to keep my wallet in the seatbelt holder above my head. When I turned to reach for the wallet, I reached up there; and this cop went nuts and threw me up against the car, and I just lost it and punched him in the face and kicked him in the family jewels. Then about three cops grabbed me and started beating the crap out of me. I had bruises all over the place the next day.

Anyway, they threw me in the back of the police car, and there was no handle on the inside of the back seat of a police car. I went ballistic trying to kick the windows out and the doors but to no avail. They took me in. They thought I was a guy. That's why they'd beaten me like that. I could have sued them for a lot of money that night. They put me in jail, and I cussed them for hours. My mother called there and told me she could hear me when she was talking to the cop on the phone. She called and told them I had two brothers that were cops, so my sister Jackie got called. She came and bailed me out; they let me go on drinking and driving, and it only cost me thirty-five dollars because of my brothers and because they figured out they just hurt a chick. And hurt I was, and I know I deserved it. So you don't have to go there. That should help you understand how I was then. I was a messed up child and young adult. I had no values and did not care about much. Well, when I got born again, that all changed. It was like someone just reached inside of me and turned the light on. I was different, and I knew it. I tried so hard to go back to what I was before I got saved, but I would say every night before I went to sleep, "God, please forgive me. Amen."

I never saw anything wrong with what I was or who I was or how I lived, and no one told me to ask for forgiveness. No one told me how I lived was wrong. I just had a new voice I had never heard before. It was the sweetest, most loving voice I had ever heard. I was so blown away by it, and he just would love me out of so much. I had no idea of where he would take me, but he never quit loving me. He never left me. He has never forsaken me. And I did not even know. God told us He will never leave us nor forsake us (Deuteronomy 31:6, NKJV).

I would be in the middle of having sex, and I would hear him. He never made me feel like I was so evil like some people do. He just talked to me. He let me know he was waiting for me, and he just would help me even when I did not have enough knowledge of him to ask. Satan tried to get me to commit suicide more than once after that, and I dealt with that a lot. Even though I was born again, the enemy was determined to kill me by my own hand. I began to hear the sound of the gun going off. I would see the back of my head being blown off. I could not stop these pictures 'cause I was not meditating on the Word. I had gotten lazy about the Word and my meditation.

Then one day it was a day service. There was an evangelist at our church. His name was Rodney Howard Brown. He was having a revival at our church, night and day meetings for about two or three weeks. I was working for Com Ed at the time, and I was working afternoons which I had disliked greatly, but I was dealing with it. It turned out to be a training ground for me. I worked with some people that were very different, but I learned to deal with a lot of different kinds of people and personalities there. Anyway I had went to a day meeting, and I had to go to work that afternoon. I sat in that meeting. I could have went to my pastor, but I did not. I thought I could deal with it, but I was losing and I knew it. That morning after praise and worship, Rodney started to talk, and he looked at us and said, "I don't know who you are, but someone is dealing with a spirit of suicide. And if you will come forth for prayer, God will set you free."

I was up front so fast I blew my own mind. I thought I was the first one to get up. This man of God laid hands on me, and I remember how strong the power was. I cried, and I sobbed. Then he laid hands on us again after service. I can tell you this, the Lord set me free that day; and any attempt of that spirit does not even light on me. I am so free from that spirit that I cannot tell you. And I will say this, God stopped me two times that I would have done it. I did not tell anyone I would have done it. God stopped me the second time when I had went to my mom's house because I knew she was not home, and I knew where she kept her gun. I went to that box and opened it. I moved the papers and looked very hard. I did not see the gun. Later I found out that gun was in that box, but I do believe that God blinded my eyes to it. Praise God. He stopped it by a miracle again. The first time was when he brought those ladies to my sister's house. Then again years later, when I had backslidden and walked away from the Lord, I am so thankful he intervened 'cause I love him so much now that I had no idea I could ever be as free as I am now. I just love him so much and what he has done in me. I will shout it from the rooftops, and some cannot handle that 'cause they still see me for what I was, but I see what God sees now, and it has taken a lot of the water of the washing of the Word which is Ephesians 5:26. I want every Christian to know one thing: if they know anything, you have got to meditate on the written Word of God to win. I would not be as free today and as changed as I am today if it was not for the written Word of God and meditating on it. The man that Satan put in this female has been erased, and the woman that God made is alive. Well, I am so thankful that God never stopped loving me, and he never stopped drawing me. He would not let me go. He gave me a pastor that would not lie to me. He gave me the Word and jerked the slack out of me and gave me the uncompromised Word of God, and he walked it out in front of me. He still does. I am so blessed to know God, and he is not a respecter of persons. What he has done for me, he will do it for you.

I want to tell so many women and men that have been taken from all their lives that God is faithful. If there is not one person who will help you or try to understand you, God knows who you are. All you have to do is run to him, and he will set you free and take you places you never thought possible. God put a dream in me that I just can only tell you that I can't keep it in. It's too big for me, but it's not too big for him. He will bring it to pass. I must get my dream to be accomplished so many can know that God is for them. I don't care where they have come from or what they have done. I am different, and I know it, but I am not special. I am just committed and driven by what he has spoken to me. When I shared it, not many were excited about it. But I am because I want people saved and helped and, most of all, free in Jesus and happy like God wants them.

I am my most blessed when I have been with the Master. There is nothing like getting alone with God, and he just keeps changing me and making me more like him. The enemy fights the hardest to keep us out of God's presence and intimacy with the King of kings.

CHAPTER 9

Mom

As I have stayed committed to the Lord and been going where I do believe the Lord placed me which is Family Harvest Church (that is the new name of the House of Glory), I have seen the Lord do much when it seemed like I was not even watching. As I have walked with the Lord and done his Word to the best of my ability, meditated on the Word, and went to church consistently, I have just changed so much. It has been so subtle. I just looked back, and I see such a difference in me and in how I see myself and how grown up I am now. And that did not happen while I was looking; it just happened.

God has had people in my life who just took care of me and loved me. And the last one had to be my mom that some things had to come from. I moved in with my mom about 1997. She was about seventy-three years old then, and she knew she did not protect and take care of me like she should have. She knew she was not a mom to me when I was growing up. She knew what my stepdad did and what my brother did was true. She had said to me so many times that she was so sorry for that; and if she had it to do all over again, she would do it differently.

I so appreciate her telling me that, and she had said it with tears. But that is not going to help a lot. It does help to know she realizes it, and it helps to know she is sorry for it; but the damage was done. Well, I guess in the last couple of years, I have seen myself grow up. I knew this was happening, but I did not realize until one night when I was talking to someone on the phone that I have grown up, and it dawned on me what had happened. My mom had been trying so hard since I moved here to take care of me. Even though it had been stuff like washing my clothes and cooking my dinner and anything else I want, she did, and just talking with her and spending time with her here and there, I have been healed inside over these years.

I can't explain it. I just know that I have gotten to know her and spent time with her and saw her try so hard to make up for things. As I have went to church consistently and meditated on God's Word, he has done something inside of me that only he could. I don't feel so lost anymore. I feel and know I am whole. God has put me back together again. In the meantime, he has taken a lost little kid and caused her to grow up, and I never thought I would. I really did not think I could ever be who I am today.

God changed me inside. He just loved me so much I could not help but change. I see me as a blessed woman whom God made me to start with. I know it has been the Word of God that has changed me. God said in his Word in Psalm 138–2b (NKJV), "God has magnified His Word even above His name."

As I have meditated on the Word of God, he has reshaped me and filled me up with himself. That is where the change takes place. Ephesians 5:26 (NKJV) says, "That He might sanctify her, having cleansed her by the washing of water with the Word."

When Jesus came, he was the Word, and he made it alive. There is no truer statement than the Word is alive! When I was taught to meditate on the Word, it placed a foundation under me that no one else could. The Word has made me who I am today.

As I have meditated on it and gotten the nectar out of it, I have been made whole. Where there is life, there is Jesus. I had to meditate on the Word of God, so he could reach inside in places only he could and change everything that was not correct inside of me. The Word is alive, and it has everything we need, but we must say it and say it and say it until we cannot say it anymore without being extremely tired of saying it.

> From the very first day, we were there, taking it all in. We heard it with our own ears, saw it with our own eyes, verified it with our own hands.
>
> The Word of Life appeared right before our eyes; we saw it happen! And now we're telling you in most sober prose that what we witnessed was, incredibly, this: The infinite Life of God himself took shape before us. (1 John 1:1–2, MSG)

Then the life of it will shape and mold and heal us everywhere we could possibly hurt. It is not dead letter. It is truly alive. I was a losing Christian like so many I know. There are so many people today who never really experienced the healing and the change that can only come from God through his Word. If he has to move heaven and hell to bring his Word to pass, he will.

I will worship toward Your holy temple and praise Your name for Your loving-kindness and for Your truth and faithfulness; for You have exalted above all else Your name and Your word and You have magnified Your word above all Your name! (Psalm 138:2, NKJV)

He has exalted his Word even above his name. God's Word will never ever fail—never ever! God saw everything that happened to me as a child, and he moved so much to get me back and heal me. There were people in my life all the time that took care of me and loved me, and maybe it did not look right sometimes. But for me, it was something I needed deep inside, and only deep calls to deep ; and I believe you cannot get much deeper than God. He searches the hearts, and he knows exactly what the deal is for all of us. When I received Him as my Lord and Savior, he was already on his way to fixing Humpty Dumpty—and only he could do it.

Living here with my mom, I have seen him do things in her too. We both have seen God do some things that we know could only come from the Father. I myself have been so changed and healed that I can only say if God can do it for me, then he can do it for anyone. He is no respecter of persons. As I have lived with my mom, I thought when I first moved back, I was doing it for her, only to find that God has done things in our relationship that only he could do. We laughed together. We have cried together. But all in all, I would give my life for her today, and I don't know what I would do without her. I look at her now, and I am so proud of her.

God has given me a love for her like I never thought I could have. All the anger is gone, and I understand her and why a lot of things were the way they were. She hid a lot of pain of her own and a lot of things she just did not understand, and she hid that as well. But as I have gotten to know her, she is a pretty special lady; and I am glad she is my mom.

She has cooked my dinners, washed my clothes, and shopped for me. She has done everything that she thought would help me, and it has done things inside of me that God knew would happen. It had to come from her, and now she is eighty years old, at least physically. But I think in her heart maybe fifty. God saw to it that this would happen and her and I could live quite happily and blessed. My mother's parents were Pentecostal preachers. They said Grandma could preach better than Grandpa. But Grandma would sit up on the pulpit and pray in the Spirit while Grandpa preached, and she would prophecy sometimes, or she would interpret what someone spoke in tongues. See, my mom was raised that way, but her mother got sick at a very young age; and she did not believe in medicine. She believed that if God wanted her healed, she would be. She would not go to the doctor, so my mom watched her die of cancer at thirty-nine years old. Mom just got angry at God and walked away from God and backslid. She used to sing with her sisters in church before her mom and dad would preach; they were in the ministry when my mom was a child. They were so poor that the church had to take an offering up for shoes for my mom, and they thought that that was okay. They did not understand the word about prosperity.

Mom came back to the Lord in 1980, and she got baptized and healed and filled with the Holy Spirit all that day. And that changed the rest of her life, and I am so thankful for that. We talked about the Lord a lot, and for a long time, she went to church 'til it got too hard for her to sit in church for too long 'cause when she went to get up, she was so stiff she could not walk. So she did not go like she used to, but she loved the Lord and watched preachers on TV. She sent her tithe to church with me, and I am glad she gave the Lord what is his because I don't ever want to live with a thief, and I have not had too because God is so good to me. He even saw to it that she would tithe because the Word is the bottom line here.

> Will a man rob or defraud God? Yet you rob and defraud me. But you say, "In what way do we rob or defraud you?" (*You have withheld your*) tithes and offerings.
>
> "You are cursed with the curse, for you are robbing me, even this whole nation. Bring all the tithes (the whole tenth of your income) into the storehouse, that there may be food in my house, and prove me now by it," says the Lord of hosts, "if I will not open the windows of heaven for you and pour you out a blessing, that there shall not be room enough to receive it."
>
> "And I will rebuke the devourer [*insects and plagues*] for your sakes and he shall not destroy the fruits of your ground, neither shall your vine drop its fruit before the time in the field," says the Lord of hosts. (Malachi 3:8–11, AMPC)

My mom had been such a blessing to me, and I cannot tell you how far God has brought me in this whole thing. He is truly a good God, and he will do whatever it takes for his kids. If he has to move heaven and hell, he will do it. My mom was a blessing, and I pray that I was a blessing to her. I can't even say that five years ago. I could have told you this is where we would be. You know, there is so much behind me and God has just took a hurting lost little girl and made her a happy, healthy, and strong woman who loves him and trusts him with all of it by his living Word that is the answer to everything, and I do mean everything.

His Word moves. It has power like you would not believe. It is alive and strong; it changes circumstances all the time, and people have it laying on their coffee tables. They just don't read it and let it change them.

> For if anyone only listens to the Word without obeying it and being a doer of it, he is like a man who looks carefully at his (*own*) natural face in a mirror;
>
> For he thoughtfully observes himself, and then goes off and promptly forgets what he was like.
>
> But he who looks carefully into the faultless law, the (*law*) of liberty, and is faithful to it and perseveres in looking into it, being not a heedless listener who forgets but an active doer (*who obeys*), he shall be blessed in his doing (his life of obedience). (James 1:23–25, AMPC)

When I began to look at the Word and listen to the Word and meditated on the Word and *did* the Word, I was changed so much from as they say: from rugs on the floor to pictures on the wall. He began to change me in ways I never thought possible. Yes, some of it hurt, but I was quite willing to go through it because I wanted to be whole. I wanted to know God intimately, and I did not want anyone between him and me. And I still don't. He has loved me like no one ever could have, and he wanted me when nobody else did. He is such a good God, and I love him so much.

My mom went to be with Jesus in August 24, 2018. My prayer for Mom was that her transition to him would be smooth and easy. She fell at age ninety-two. She was healthy physically with a little dementia but physically good. She walked fine and got tired quickly, but she did not need a cane or a walker for the most part. When she fell, she broke her hip and right arm, actually shattered the bone in the arm under her right shoulder. They did surgery right away on both, and the doctor came out of surgery and said her arm was so bad it looked like she had fallen down three flights of stairs. We were walking into a place where they had a big rug between the set of sliding glass doors, and her foot got caught on the corner of the rug. I could not stop her from falling, and she fell very fast. I carried guilt over her falling because she was with me. I just wish I could have caught her somehow. I had to get on the Word about that too. Romans 8:1a (NKJV) says, "There is therefore now no condemnation for those who are in Christ Jesus."

I miss my mom big-time, but I know my Father has her, and she is just fine. One day we will reunite and never part again. I got to be with her when she went to go be with the Lord. She said to me the day before she went home that God was waiting for her. She fought hard and had a very strong will to live, but her arm, she could not use at all. She was right-handed, and she could not walk without a walker. Really even then, she could hardly walk. She was in a wheel-chair the last three months after she fell; and I knew she would not want to live that way. We got to bring her home the last six weeks of her life. I really wanted her here, so we turned her living room into a big hospital room. We got a hospital bed for her and everything we needed. God provided all the help we needed. I worked full-time, so I needed a lot of help. God put it in my heart to bring her home, and he provided everything.

My sister Jeanie came sometimes three times a week, and my niece Vicki came a lot. Cheryl, one of my best friends, moved in with us when Mom started with the dementia. God is faithful. The day Mom went home to heaven, I came home from work, and I was sitting with Mom next to her bed. She said she was ready. I said, "Mom, are you angry at anyone?" She said "no." I asked her to pray with me and just make sure she was good with the Lord, which she was. She mumbled some, and it sounded like she said, "I love you."

I asked her if that was what she said. She said "yes." I told her, "I love you too, Mom." I pulled her hand close to my heart. I put my hand on her head, and we started praying. I knew she wanted to go home. She had been asking me to take her there. I finally realized she just was tired and done here. I started praying, "Take her home, Father. She is ready." After about less than five minutes, she went to be with Jesus.

I did not want her to go by herself, and she did not. God takes care of every detail, and I am sure she had prayed not to be alone. I got to be with her and hold her and love her. I did not want to go in a convalescent home. I wanted her taken care of with love, and that is what she got. My mom loved Jesus, and I am thankful she repented and got her life right. That could only happen because she made Jesus her Lord and Savior, and the Holy Spirit moved in and changed her too.

CHAPTER 10

My Foundation

Jesus Christ is my foundation—his Word, blood, and body! He is and will always be my everything, my rock, my strong tower, and my love.

As I have grown in God, I have seen him do so much inside of me. He has changed me inside and out, and when you are changing on the inside, the outside shows it. And it shows it before you even realize it's happening, which is kind of cool because then you know it's not you trying to change. It's just God's Word happening. You cannot get around God and not get better.

He will bring you up if you will let him. He is a good God, and he loves his children very much. Every one of us is special to him, and he lets you know it. He has numbered the hairs on our heads. He has etched our faces in the palms of his hands. He said it, and I believe it with everything in me. God gets all the glory, the honor, and the praise for all the good in my life. Coming from the background of homosexuality can be very tough for a person who is born again because the enemy has a lot of ammo. Believe it or not, it can come from the place we might least expect it from, like

Christians. I know that might be hard to believe but it's true, I guess you could call it friendly fire but it can be a lot worse than dying cause now you get to stay alive and hear people say things that they don't think you heard. Unfortunately, you did, and you get the looks from those same people.

You see, they can fall in adultery or stealing like they used to, but if you fall in homosexuality, now you are so much worse than anyone else 'cause they don't understand something they could never fall in. I suppose it's like that with other stuff, but it really sticks out with sexual perversion 'cause people think they are an authority on things they don't have a clue about. Sorry for sounding so critical, but I see the hurt on people's faces when they have to deal with the judgment and the loud quietness of someone's glance because I have felt the pain of such glances. I do not condone homosexuality any more, but I know the pain and the loneliness of people not letting you in anywhere because they think you might go after them when it's the same thing as heterosexuals do.

For some reason, people have homosexuals and pedophiles mixed up. They could not be any farther apart, except for the fact the a pedophile may have caused someone to be a homosexual instead of making them what they were. It is said that someone who has been molested as a child will either do what was done to them, or they will despise it. I am glad I have not ever had that temptation, and I am thankful I never will. My foundation and what has changed me the most is God's Word. When God's Word says it is alive, it truly is. When Jesus came and walked on the earth, he brought that life. When he died on the cross and was resurrected, he made the Word breath like we do. The Word is alive in us, and that can only happen when you give your meditation to it; it will wash you inside.

The Word is so alive that you can meditate and say out loud one Scripture for months, and it will do things inside you that can only be from God. I remember when Dr. Robb Thompson first taught me to meditate on 2 Corinthians 5:21. It's about me being the righteousness of God. I remember getting it in my spirit and thinking about it and saying it and just pondering it and sometimes even saying it before getting around some Christians who just always made me feel like I just should not be there at church, that is.

I would have to say it at least the last five minutes of my drive to church just to get myself in the door 'cause the voices of the enemy would be screaming in my ear, "You don't belong there. You're not ever going to be good enough. They don't like you there. They are just faking liking you. You are a square peg trying to fit into a round hole." The shame and guilt of my past would flood my soul. And I can tell you this: without the Word, I would have buckled no doubt.

God gave me a gift of a man named Dr. Robb Thompson who taught me how to meditate on the Word day and night. He taught me what so many preachers I had heard just did not ever know, so they could not teach it. God knew exactly what I needed, and he sent me to this church. I believe if God had not intervened, I would not have ever succeeded in him I had too much against me. Without the supernatural power of the Word, I could not have withstood the enemies' darts of failure, compromise, and straight-up sin unto death. I believe I became a believer when I truly began to stand on the Word of God. Yes, I believed I was saved. But it stopped there. I had no structure of the Word of God, no power of his Word, and no change could have taken place. If it had not been for people giving me the Word and never ever giving up on me, I can tell you this, quitting would have been a lot easier.

I know my pastor and his wife, Linda Thompson, prayed and stood for me more than anyone I know of. Linda is five feet and three quarters of an inch tall and probably weighs about ninety pounds or so. I will tell you this, I am sure she is taller than the Green Giant in the Spirit. These people stand like no one else. I know they are tough, and it is because of the Word in their lives. I am very thankful for Pastor Robb and Linda Thompson. I don't think they will really know what they did for me until the rewards are handed out in heaven because I think it was a very big job they had before them where I was concerned. They endured a lot, but they stood and kept loving me, sometimes more love than I wanted. I am thankful for every bit of it. I believe one of the first Scriptures I was taught was 2 Corinthians 5:21 (NKJV) that says: "For He made Him Who Knew no sin to be sin for us, that we might become the Righteousness of God in Him."

Now when I learned that Jesus took it all, every stinking sin I could commit and that he was sinless but loved me enough to take the cross and endure the cross, I actually meditated long enough to believe he did that.

I was so broken by that fact that he could love me that much. That alone changed even how I was myself. You see, when you are told as a child that you are stupid which was by my stepdad and then my own dad would say I was a bum and would always be a bum and his pet name for me was son of a——and you can fill in the rest, then it is quite hard to believe anyone would love me or care about me, let alone die for me on the cross and take the beating of his life for me. I mean, I was told some of this stuff so much I get all warm and fuzzy when I hear it. I cannot tell you what the love of God has made me today, but it is a whole lot better than the people who took everything from me. That is probably why

I love children so much today because I understand so much more than I can articulate to you.

Jesus is my everything. I need him so much. I love him with everything I am. My heart calls out to him, and he responds every time. No one will ever know what he means to me today. Sure, I have failed him, but I am thankful he just would not let me stay down. I do believe if you get up one more time than you fall, you will make it. You know, Jesus walked this earth as a real man. He knows every pain we could possibly endure; there is nothing that I could possibly deal with that he does not know. I believe he went through every one of them I could ever have, and he will not ever fail me for that reason. So many of us don't spend time in his Word to see what he did for us. And there is so much power there and so much change there that if we will let the water of the washing of the Word get inside where it can literally wash us day after day, taking the Holy Ghost cleanser, and doing a scrub job in there, one day you just look back and look at all that junk. It's just gone. What a wonderful God we serve. If you will just take the Word and the water of the washing of the Word, Ephesians 5:26 says, "And let the Lord cleanse you." God has already done his part. He gave us his Son, Jesus, and the New Testament written in his blood. How much more does he have to do?

> I have been crucified with Christ; For it is no longer I who live but there lives in me Christ and the life I now live I live through faith in the Son of God who loves me and has given Himself for me. (Galatians 2:20, NKJV)

My old self was crucified with Him that
the body of sin could be done away with,
that I would no longer be a slave unto
sin. (Romans 6:6)

May I never boast except the cross of my
Lord Jesus, through which the world has
been crucified to me, and I to the world.
(Galatians 6:14, NIV)

Therefore, If anyone is in Christ, he is
a new creation; old things have passed
away behold all things have become new.
(2 Corinthians 5:17, NKJV)

You are already clean because of the word
I have spoken to you. (John 15:3, NKJV)

Judy's Version: "I am morally clean, pure, sinless, and
unstained because of the Word that had been spoken to me"
(JLZV).

These Scriptures changed me on the inside. They healed
me in places no one else could have. That's why he gave us
Psalm 138:2 to show how important the Word is to our very
survival as Christians.

Satan can take his best shot; and still, he loses because
God is the boss. If we will heed his Word, we cannot lose.
God desired fellowship with us, or he wouldn't have done
what he did to get us back. He wants intimacy with us. He
loves when we take time with him or should I say when we
make time for him. He will never force himself on anyone.
He is a gentleman.

There is no one else like him, *no one*! No matter how long it takes, maybe one year, maybe twenty-five years, he will do what you need him to. We just have to stay in the place of obedience, and we will win. I will never be the same. He has taken a hurting, empty little girl and changed her into a whole complete woman. That took some doing but only he could do it. I remember when I read Numbers 23:19 that God is not a man that he should lie. Praise God he cannot lie. He is bound by his Word, and he will not break his Word. Remember you are only as good as your Word. God will do what he said, and you can take that to any bank. Psalm 138:2 (NKJV) says: "For You magnified Your Word above all Your name." That means that if he has to move heaven and hell, he will do it to do what he said. I was a child in a full-grown body. I stopped growing somewhere before adolescence. I am not sure where, but I know I was a child inside. On top of that, I was crippled, but I sure would never admit it nor could I see it. Everyone always thinks it's so cute when an adult is into cartoons. Well, most of the time, there is a problem. There is just no one who will admit it, or no one cares to deal with it mainly because they just don't know how. But God knows how and where. He will meet you right where you are, and he will love you like no one ever could. He will take you when no one else wants you, and he will fix everything inside of you if you will let him.

I stand today free from homosexuality, drug addiction, drunkenness, insecurity, and fornication. Jesus healed me spiritually, mentally, emotionally, and sexually. When I look back at that mess I was and look at me now, I look in the mirror. I have to say, "Who is that?" Then the Word of God comes up inside of me and Galatians 2:20,6:14, Romans 6:6 Proverbs 23:7, Philippians 3:9–10, and Colossians 1:22, and so very much more. That is who I am.

You get saved by praying this: Jesus come into my heart. I repent of my sin, and I make you the Lord of my life. I believe that you went to the cross for me and took every sin I could do, and your blood washed me clean. And go tell someone. Romans 10:10 tells us to "believe in our heart and confess it with our mouth." If you're having a problem believing, ask God to help you with your unbelief, and he will. God's desire is for not one to perish. His love is more than we can fathom. God loves *you*! I am living proof. God bless you.

ABOUT THE AUTHOR

I live in Northern Illinois. I have an associate's degree in theology. I am a member of Calvary church. I teach in one of their outreach ministries. I work full-time as a quality technician. I work in a metrology lab. The Lord opened that door for me; it is a good job.

He knows what is good for us better than we do. I have family and two dogs that I love and am just blessed. Just a note: I have never met a stranger. I love to tell people about Jesus and pray for them to get free. Forgiveness is not a line we cross; it is a road we take. We must stay on that road.

People are the only reason Jesus went to the cross. If you have never asked Jesus to be your Lord and Savior, then let's pray: Jesus, I ask you into my heart. I make you the Lord of my life. I ask you to cleanse me of my sins and make me who you want me to be. I believe that you were crucified for my sin. And on the third day, you were raised and are at the right hand of the Father. In Jesus's name I pray. Amen.

Now go tell someone you just got saved. Confession of Jesus is a great thing. God bless you.